Bruno Munari's

ABC

DEDICATION

He who buys this book
may make a dedication
to the child who receives it

_____

_____

Picture books by Bruno Munari

seuil
chronicle

ABC

by
Bruno
Munari

Originally published in the United States in 1960
by The World Publishing Company.

Copyright © 1960 by Bruno Munari.
All rights reserved Maurizio Corraini srl - Italy.

For the present edition in North America
Copyright © 2003 by Editions du Seuil.

Manufactured in Italy.

Library of Congress Catalog Card Number 2002156745
ISBN: 2-02-061075-2

Distributed in Canada by Raincoast Books
9050 Shaughnessy Street, Vancouver, British Columbia V6P 6E5

10 9 8 7 6 5 4 3 2 1

Chronicle Books LLC
85 Second Street, San Francisco, California 94105

www.chroniclekids.com

A

an Ant

on an Apple

a Blue Butterfly

B

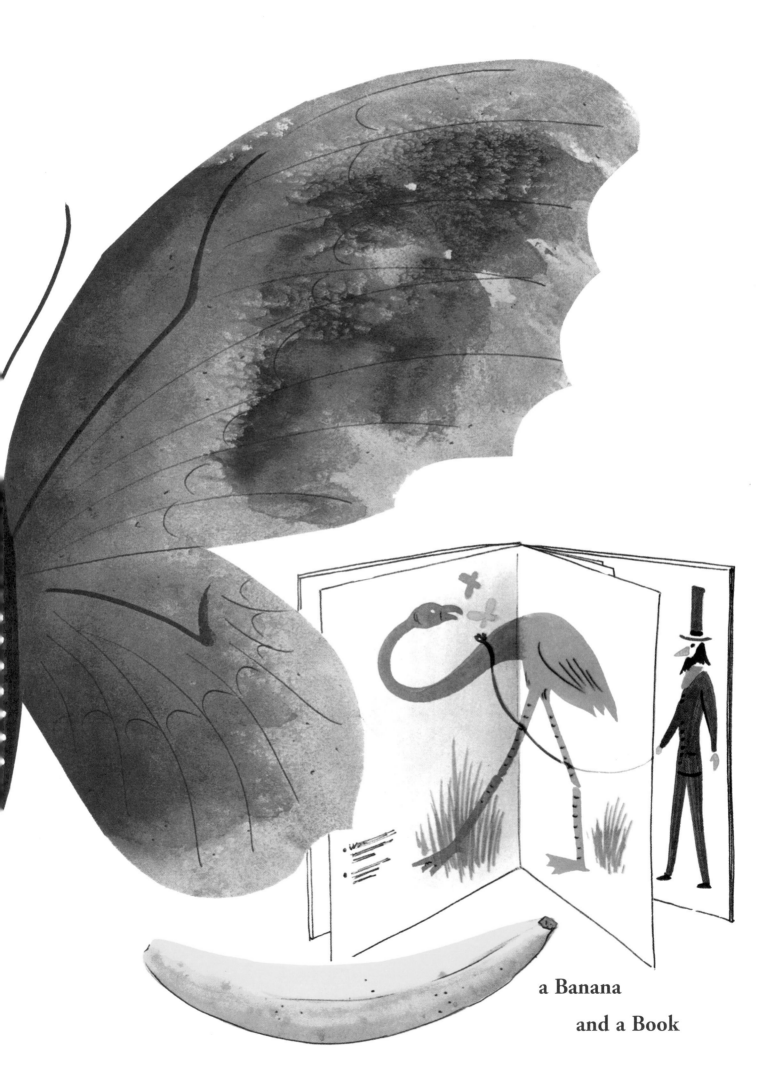

a Banana

and a Book

a Crow

on a Cup

a Candle

and a Cat in a Cage

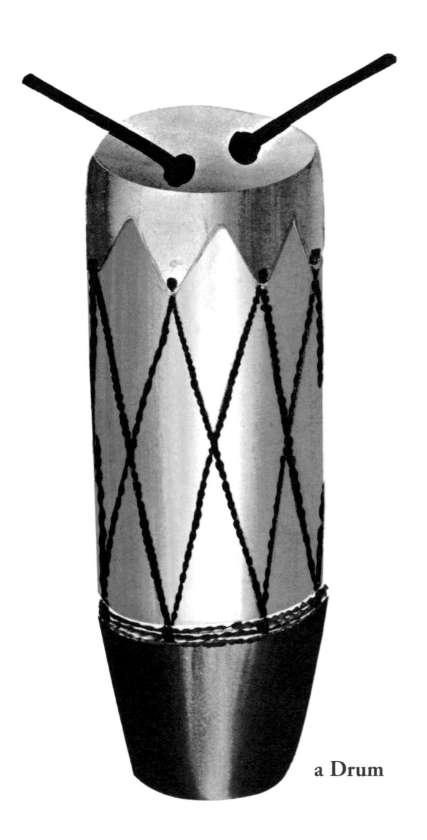

a Drum

a Dog
and his Dish
outside a Door

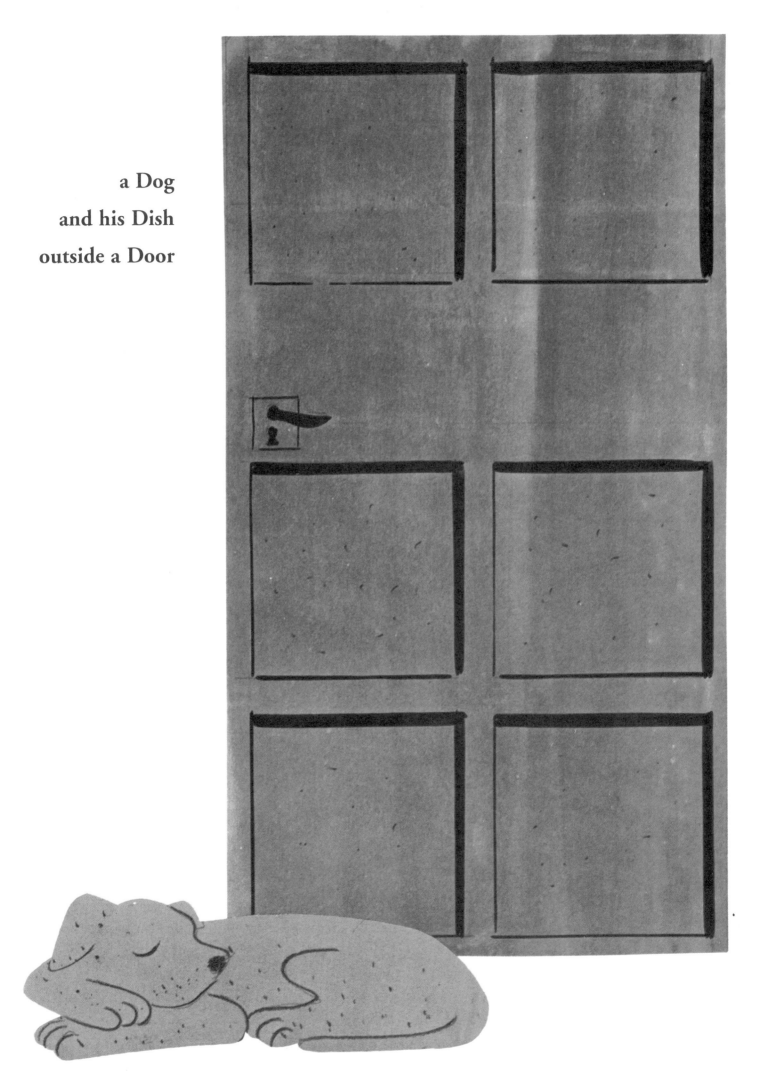

an Elephant

an Egg

an Eye
and an Ear

E

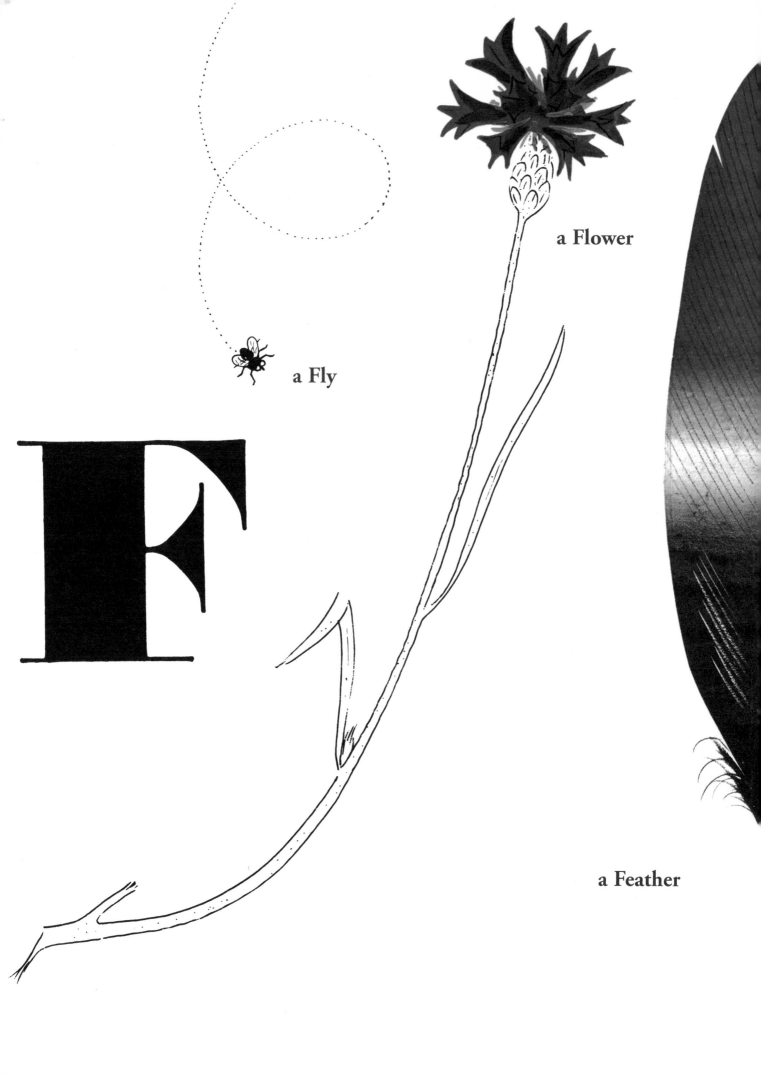

a Flower

a Fly

F

a Feather

more Flies

and a Fish

G

Glasses in Green Grass

still another fly!

and a Gift for you

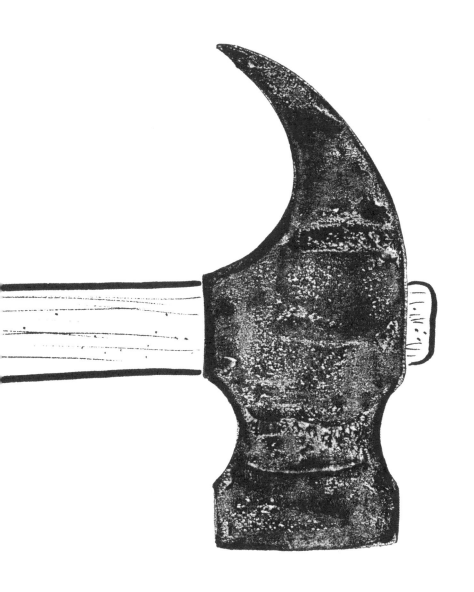

a Hammer
over a Hat

look out, fly!

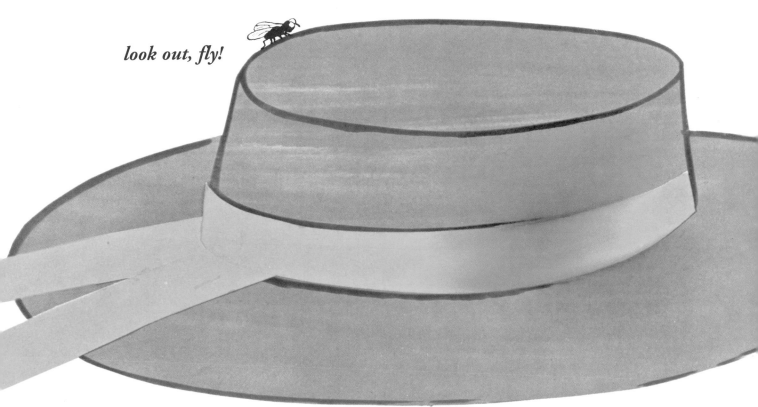

I

shoo, fly!

lots of
Ice Cream

a Juggler

a Knothole
between a Key
and a Knife

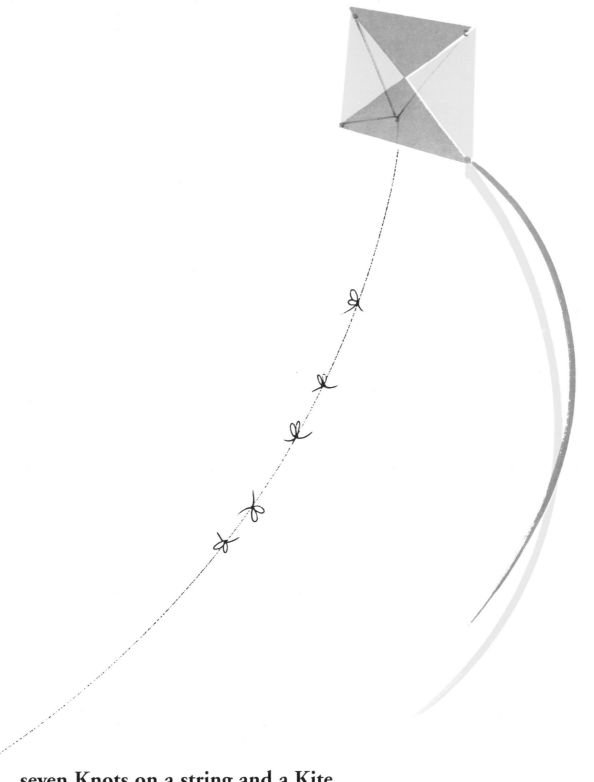

seven Knots on a string and a Kite

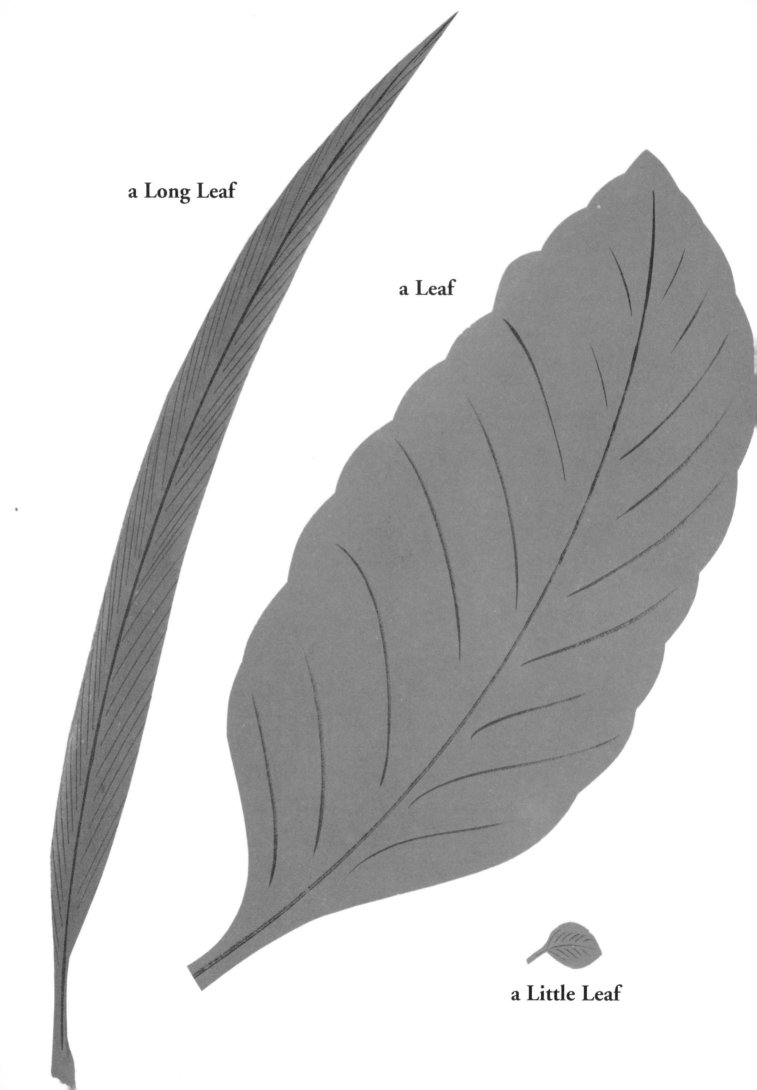

a Long Leaf

a Leaf

a Little Leaf

L

and a Lemon

a Match

M

a Monkey

and a Mouse

No bird in the Nest

Nuts on a Nail

an Owl

and an Orange

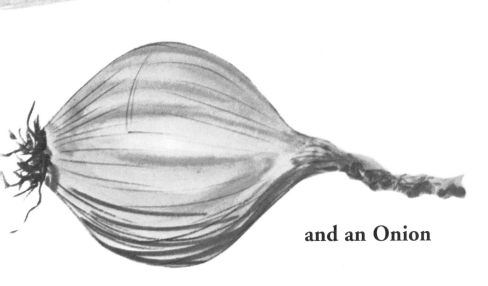

and an Onion

a Piano

a Package

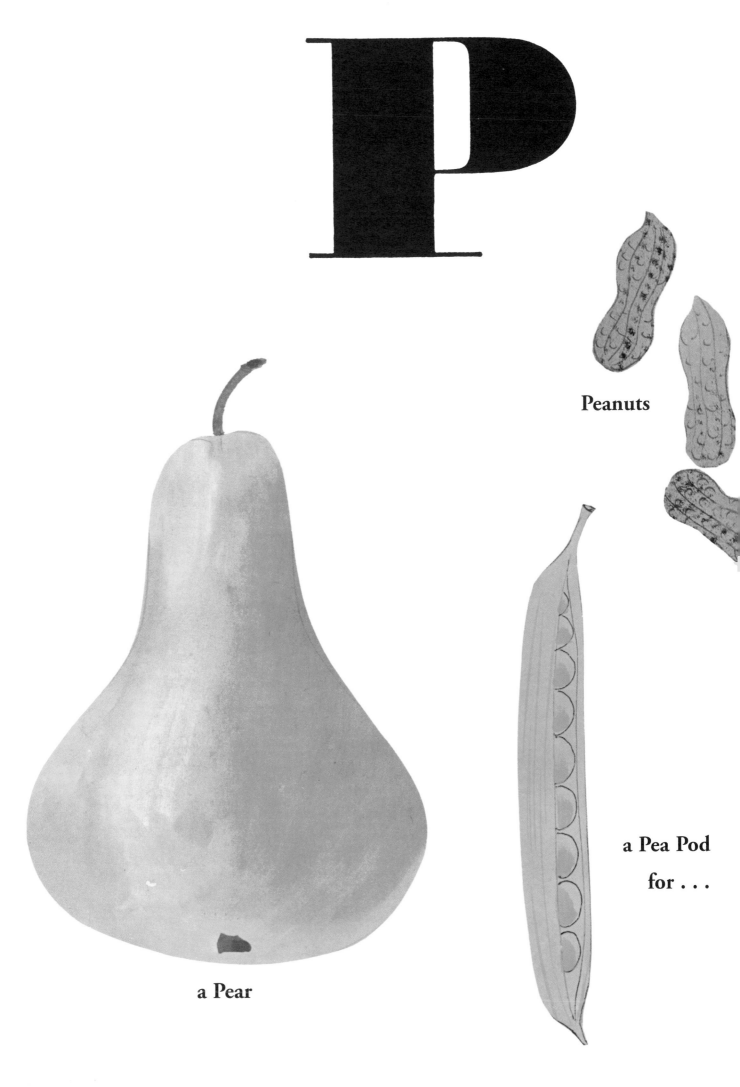

P

Peanuts

a Pear

a Pea Pod
for . . .

a Quail

a Rose

and a Red Ribbon

a Sack
of Stars
and Snow
for
Santa Claus

STOP

and a Sign

all kinds of Shells

even a Ship

and a Stone

T

a Trumpet

a Ticket

a Telephone

an Umbrella Up

and an Umbrella
Under the Umbrella

a fly on a Voyage

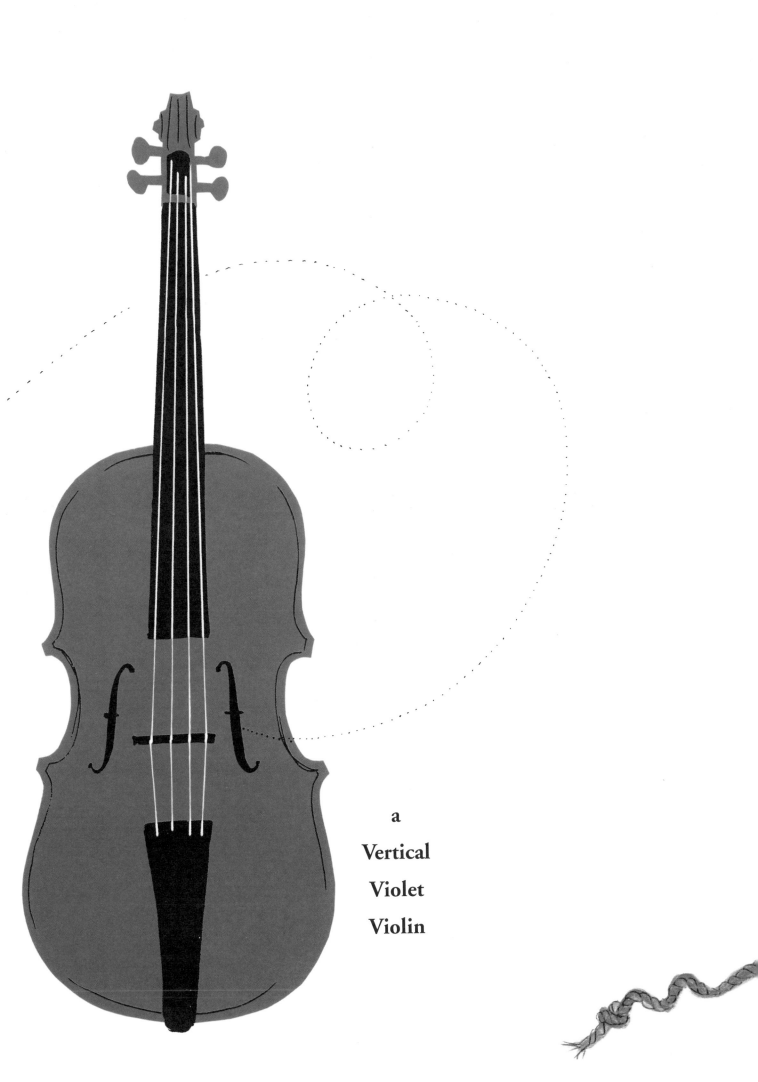

a
Vertical
Violet
Violin

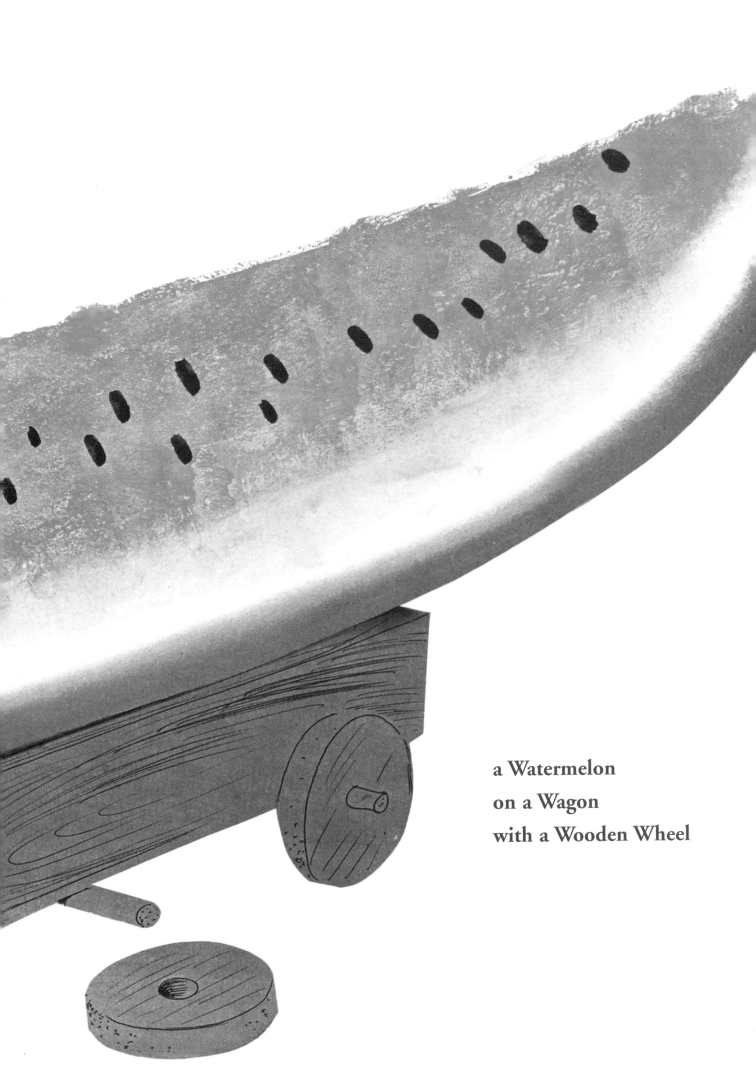

a Watermelon
on a Wagon
with a Wooden Wheel

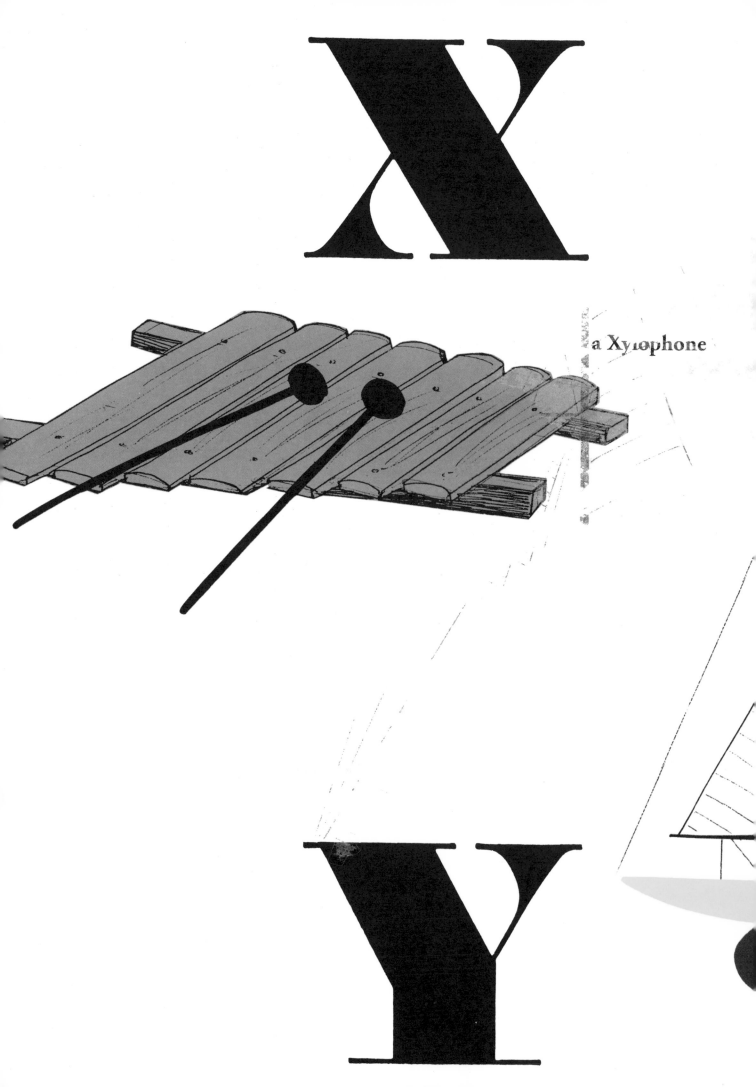

a Xylophone

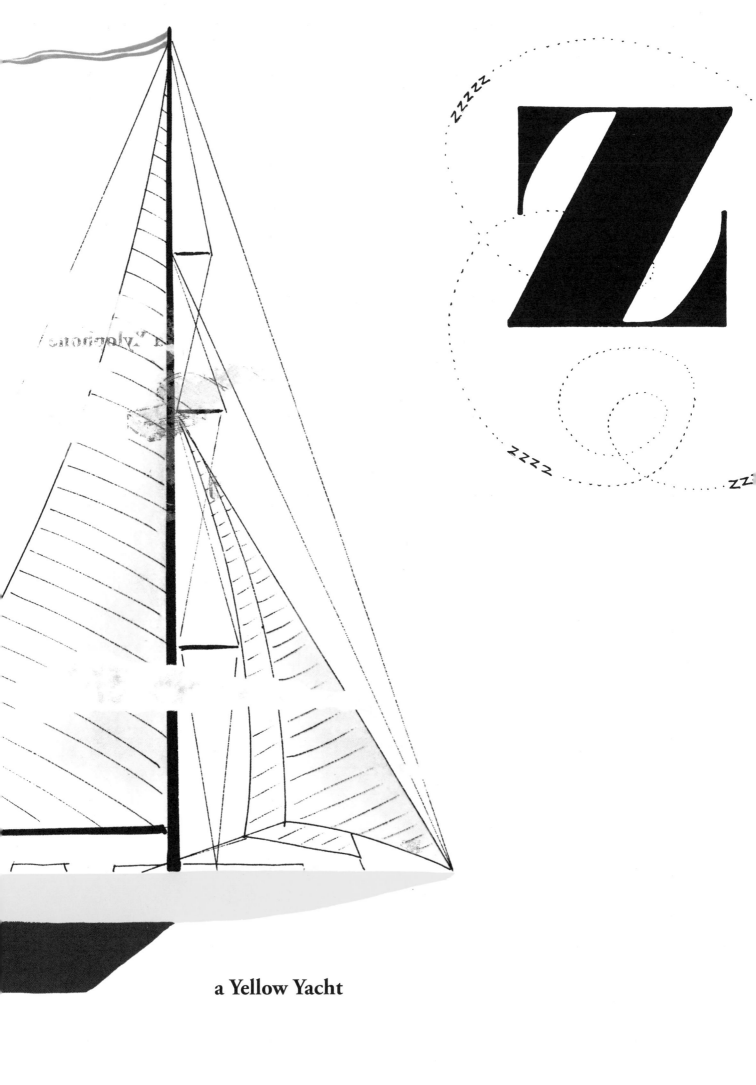

a Yellow Yacht

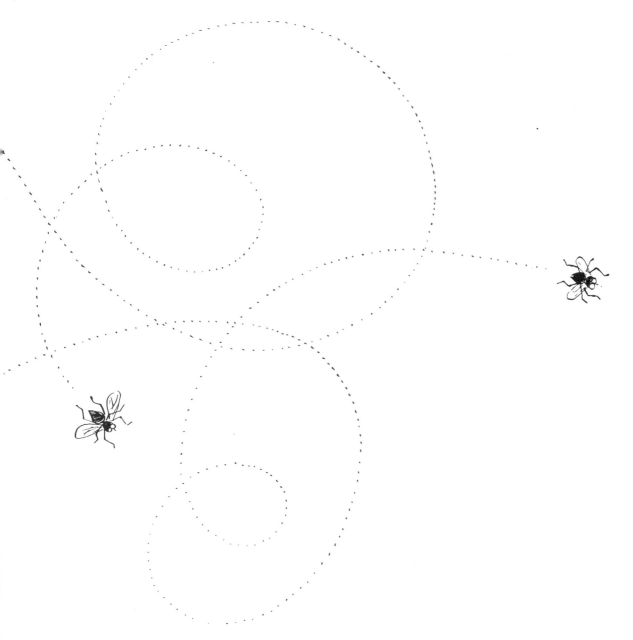

a fly going Zzzz. . . .